STORAGE

STORAGE

Edited by Cristina Paredes Benítez

COLLINS DESIGN

An Imprint of HarperCollinsPublishers

STORAGE: GOOD IDEAS
Copyright © 2007 by COLLINS DESIGN and LOFT Publications

HarperCollins books may be purchased for educational, business, or sales promotional use.
For information, please write: Special Markets Department, HarperCollins Publishers,
10 East 53rd Street, New York, NY 10022.

English language edition first published in 2007 by:
Collins Design
An Imprint of HarperCollins*Publishers*
10 East 53rd Street
New York, NY 10022
Tel.: (212) 207-7000
Fax: (212) 207-7654
collinsdesign@harpercollins.com
www.harpercollins.com

Distributed throughout the world by:
HarperCollins*Publishers*
10 East 53rd Street
New York, NY 10022
Fax: (212) 207-7654

Packaged by:
Loft Publications
Via Laietana, 32 4º, of. 92
08003 Barcelona, Spain
Tel.: +34 932 688 088
Fax: +34 932 687 073
www.loftpublications.com

Editor: Cristina Paredes Benítez
Editorial Assistant: Claire Dalquié
Texts: Francesc Zamora, Cristina Paredes Benítez
Translation: Bridget Vranckx, Jay Noden
Art Director: Mireia Casanovas Soley
Layout: Nil Solà

Library of Congress Cataloging-in-Publication Data

Paredes, Cristina.
    Storage : good ideas / Cristina Paredes.
        p. cm.
    ISBN-13: 978-0-06-114420-2 (pbk.)
    ISBN-10: 0-06-114420-7 (pbk.)
    1. Storage in the home. 2. Interior decoration. I. Title.

NK2117.S8P37 2007
648'.8—dc22

2007008091

Printed in Spain by Anman Gràfiques del Vallès
DL: B-27150-07

First printing, 2007

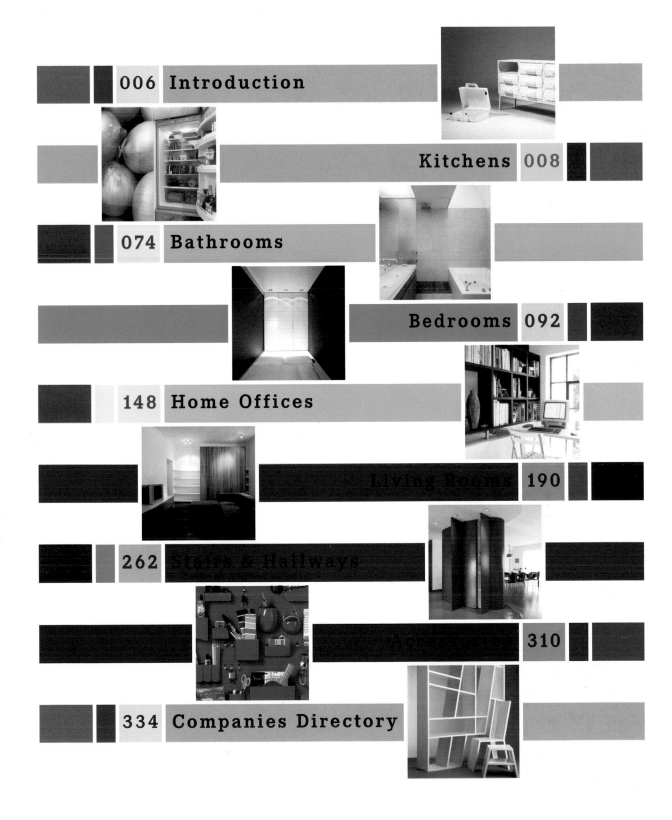

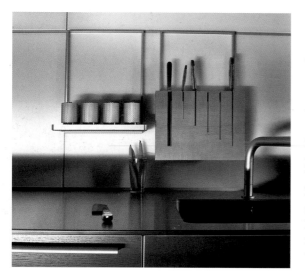

Organizing a home is complex. Each room has its own function, its own needs, and its own objects. As people accumulate more, the adage "a place for everything and everything in its place" rings true. The problem: How do you keep many diverse things well organized and within easy reach? Lots of good storage is the answer, and designers are rising to the challenge, producing attractive, innovative solutions.

In the well-conceived living room these days, you might find movable partitions hiding bookcases and separating spaces. As city dwellings become smaller, a bedroom might simply be a luxe mattress atop a large storage platform. Hallways and other forgotten spaces are being fitted with rows of closets so discrete they're barely perceptible. Bookcases minimize their footprint and rise to the ceiling. And the major kitchen functions can now fit into one freestanding island, so beautiful it resembles a work of art.

Introduction

Decor can also present opportunities for improving storage. For example, kitchens can be decorated to create clean, airy environments despite their large size, offices or dressing rooms can avoid appearing overloaded despite the large volume of items stored there, and single spaces can be designed to carry out several functions at once.

Storage explores options available in each major space in the house: living rooms, kitchens, bathrooms, bedrooms, home offices, and halls and stairways. The final chapter looks at some of the more innovative storage accessories available today. Have a look; you might just find the solution you've been hoping for.

Kitchens

Architect: AvroKO Arquitectos *Localization:* New York, N.Y., U.S. *Photography:* © Gogortza & Llorella

COOK BETTER: ideas for a more flavorful life

Kitchens are special places in the house. Their functions are clearly defined and mark the need for basic elements such as installations for water and gas, taps, and waterresistant materials. Kitchen furniture must be adaptable to the space available and provide easy access to all the objects found inside, such as cutlery or kitchen equipment. Today's cupboards, drawers, shelves, and other storage modules are being adapted to contemporary needs and offer increasingly practical solutions. Modular furniture is becoming more and more versatile, incorporating elements with wheels that make the space more flexible and accessories for organizing drawers or objects, such as spices or kitchen knives. The decorative style of the kitchen, and the materials and colors used, lend it personality and allow an open kitchen to be integrated with the living room, or the cupboards to go unnoticed, despite their capacity for storing a large number of objects. The kitchen has evolved a lot, from being a place for servants in bourgeois houses of the 20th century to being the center of the home. Because of today's pace of living, the living room is no longer the center of family reunions. As kitchens are now the center of our homes, they need to be practical as well as welcoming. In many cases they need to be designed to be able to accommodate both the kitchen and dining room in one room, while in others the limits between the kitchen and living area is eliminated to create a large open space.

The custom design and mobility of some of the pieces in this kitchen creates an extremely flexible space.

Architect: McDowell & Benedetti *Localization:* London, UK *Photography:* © Jordi Miralles

Taking advantage of generous ceiling height, the architects built a platform of solid wood planks over the kitchen to make room for an office. In the kitchen, all the storage is concealed behind richly textured wood paneling.

The space under the stairway allows for some storage space, while the front paneling serves as a guardrail.

Architect: Cristina Fernández, Ignasi Pérez Arnal / Labb Arquitectura *Localization:* Granollers, Spain *Photography:* © Gogortza & Llorella

The kitchen island provides convenient and efficient storage space, leaving the back wall available for the pantry, integrated refrigerator and freezer, built-in oven, and microwave.

The wine rack is a storage space which doubles as a decorative element in the kitchen.

Interior design: **Albert Aubach** *Localization:* **Viladomat, Spain** *Photography:* © **José Luis Hausmann**

The wood of the cupboards contrasts with the original stone walls, creating a cozy atmosphere.

Architect: James Slade Localization: New York, N.Y., U.S. Photography: © Jordi Miralles

The inside of the cupboards shows through the transparent glass, without displaying the objects completely.

The kitchen here is an independent element within an existing building. The pantry slides out from behind the back wall of the kitchen as if to compartmentalize the space.

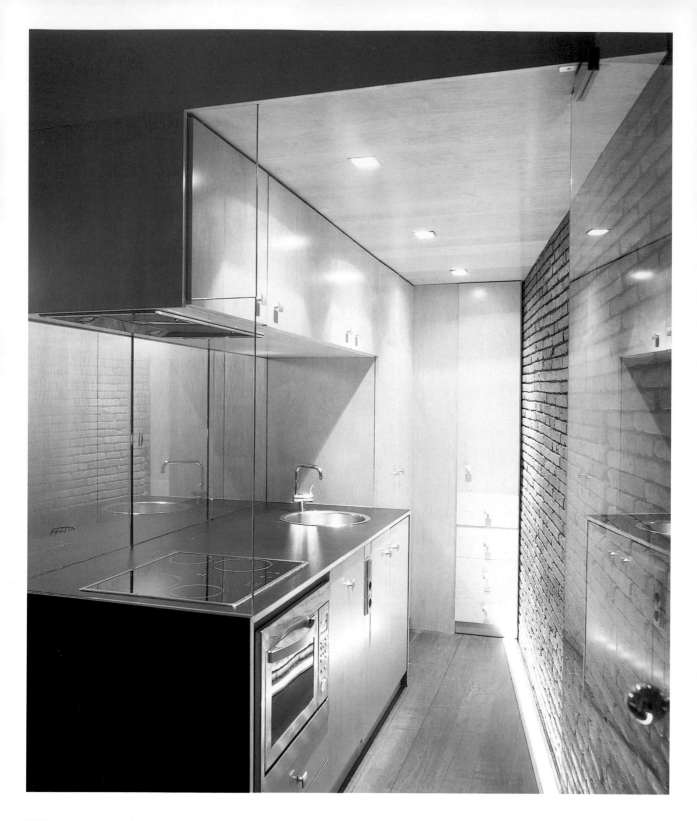

Architect: Daylin Torres / Cru 2001 *Localization:* Barcelona, Spain *Photography:* © Gogortza & Llorella

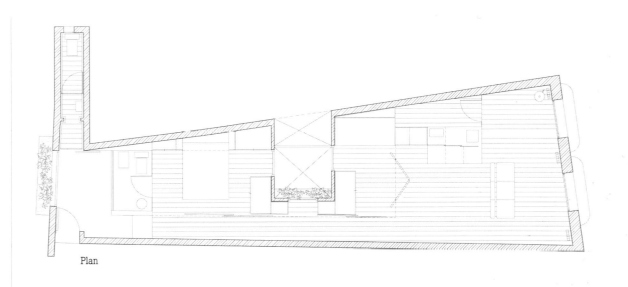

Plan

The kitchen has sculptural elements and practical solutions such as the possibility of opening the piece of furniture from both sides and placing the fridge for the wine near the dining room.

Architect: **Feyferlik-Fritzer** *Localization:* **Vienna, Austria** *Photography:* © Paul Ott, Graz

A storage niche at the front of the island comes in handy for those seated at the table.

The kitchen's work surface can be used as a study table, which is an original solution for small spaces.

Architect: **Unknown** *Localization:* **Madrid, Spain** *Photography:* © **Luis Hevia**

A platform on top of the kitchen provides additional storage space for possessions not needed on a daily basis, while the front wall of the bar is used as an area to display art.

The space beneath the stairs has been used to store kitchen furniture of different heights.

Architect: Roger Bellera *Localization:* Spain *Photography:* © Jordi Miralles

Architect: Unknown *Localization:* Unknown *Photography:* © K. Rogers / H&L / Inside / COVER

The shelf under the kitchen island provides easy access to kitchen utensils or appliances too large to fit in a cabinet.
Tall pantry pullouts built into one wall are an efficient way to make good use of the space.

■■■ *Architect:* Ramón Pintó *Localization:* Cabrera, Spain *Photography:* © Jordi Miralles

The combination of doors and drawers of different heights makes room for all kitchen utensils.

Overhead cabinets hang down from the ceiling, creating the interesting effect of a floating element.

Architect: Hofman Dujardin Architecten *Localization:* Amsterdam, the Netherlands *Photography:* © Matthijs van Roon

This futuristic kitchen element fits in the space like a piece of art, revealing its functions very subtly.

Architect: Alfons Soldevila *Localization:* Alella, Spain *Photography:* © Jordi Miralles

Undoubtedly, an important goal in kitchen design is to always search for a better marriage of aesthetics and function

Architect: Juan Luis Madariaga *Localization:* Spain *Photography:* © Jordi Miralles

This kitchen table can be moved away if more room is needed, via a rail which is made up of the work bench and the cupboard doors.

Architect: Raúl Campderrich / Air Projects *Localization:* Barcelona, Spain *Photography.* © Jordi Miralles

Interior design: **Francesc Rifé** *Localization:* **Barcelona, Spain** *Photography:* © **Gogortza & Llorella**

A tinted glass panel slides over to close the kitchen pass-through and enclose the adjacent room.

The divider between the kitchen and dining area provides a place to install electrical outlets above the countertop.

Interior design: Jesyca Delgado Fritz *Localization:* **Barcelona, Spain** *Photography:* © José Luis Hausmann

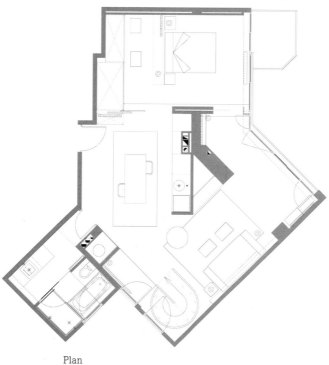

Plan

Architect: **Pilar Líbano** *Localization:* **Barcelona, Spain** *Photography:* © **Gogortza & Llorella**

Because of the reduced dimensions, the kitchen has been integrated into the decorative theme of the apartment.

Architect: Silvia Via *Localization:* Barcelona, Spain *Photography:* © Gogortza & Llorella

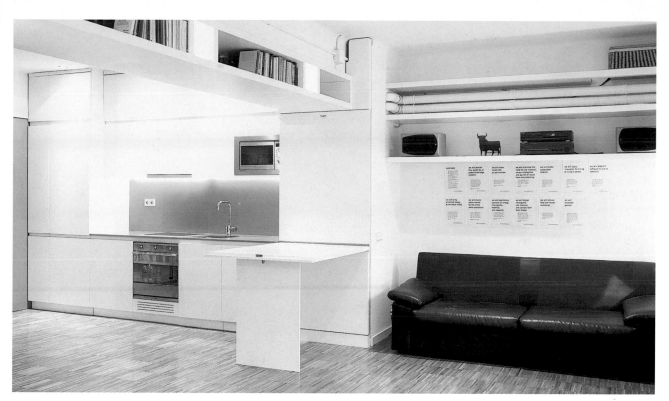

The challenge in small apartments is how to make the most of what little storage space there is. Overhead bookshelves and folding tables are clever storage solutions in this well-conceived design.

Open shelves can become an interesting compositional element and a reflection of the occupant's personality.

Architect: Unknown *Localization:* Denmark *Photography:* © K. AHM / House of Pictures / Inside / Cover

Architect: James Slade *Localization:* New York, N.Y., U.S. *Photography:* © Jordi Miralles

Some thought put into the design of custom-made cabinetry can make a difference when maximizing the amount of storage space becomes critical. The result is a compact kitchen with great capacity.

Architect: **Unknown** *Localization:* **Denmark**
Photography: © B.W. Drejer / House of Pictures / Inside / Cover

Simple, easy, inexpensive, and charming storage is a homey alternative to bright, sleek, expensive, and sophisticated schemes.

Company: Elmar Cucine *Photography:* © Elmar Cucine

Furniture & Accessories Design

Kitchen design has become a highly specialized field, where designers focus on making the kitchen both functional and appealing. These days, even chandeliers are welcome.

Company: Elmar Cucine *Photography:* © Elmar Cucine

The kitchen has evolved over the years and is now a space where the family gets together. This kitchen has an extendable table, which can be adjusted depending on the space needed.

Company: Elmar Cucine Photography: © Elmar Cucine

Designers strive to find a balance between aesthetics and durable surfaces. Glossy stainless steel countertops, a popular choice, clean easily.

Company: Sub-Zero Wolf *Photography:* © Sub-Zero Wolf

The quality of the manufacturer is uncovered in the quality of the materials used and the way the furniture adapts to available space and the needs of every user.

Company: Sub-Zero Wolf *Photography:* © Sub-Zero Wolf

Wine coolers are becoming an indispensible piece of equipment in today's kitchens. Living habits have evolved such that the kitchen is no longer the homemaker's exclusive domain; it is also now a place to entertain and socialize.

Company: Orit *Photography:* © Yael Pincus

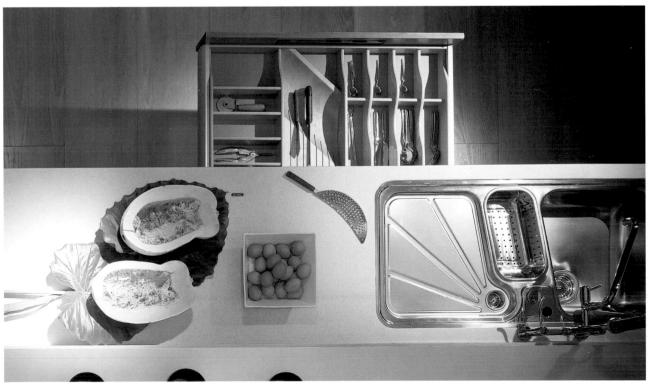

Special storage drawers for kitchen utensils, equipment and spices are becoming more and more inventive

Company: Bulthaup *Photography:* © Bulthaup

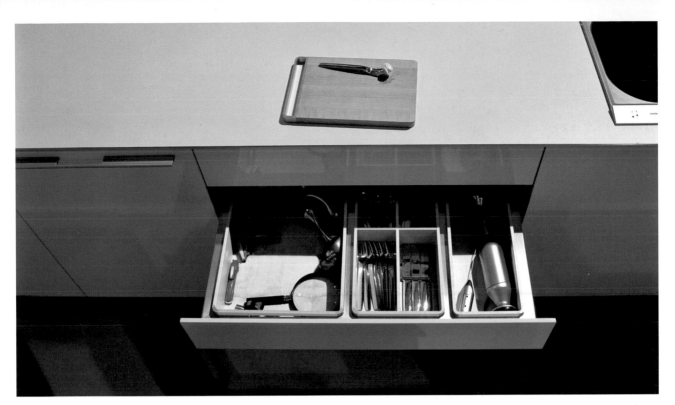

Company: Bulthaup *Photography:* © Bulthaup

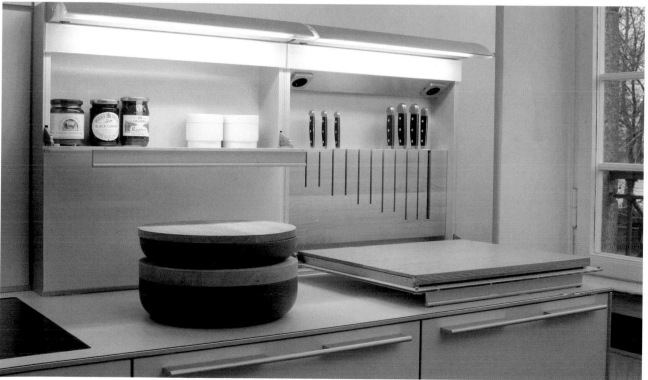

Concealed storage for appliances, under-cabinet lighting and fold-down cutting boards are increasingly important kitchen components. The way they are integrated into the design contributes to making a highly functional kitchen.

Bathrooms

Previous page | *Architect:* Pedro Mora *Location:* Guadalajara, Spain *Photography:* © Luis Hevia

GROOM BETTER: solutions
to help kick-start the day

The bathroom is one of the rooms that has a specific and special use. Therefore the need for storage here is different than the other rooms in the house. Bathrooms are usually smaller than kitchens and bedrooms and distribution of its elements, such as the toilet, sink, and bath, is fundamental in obtaining a well-organized space. Moreover, this room is frequently used (especially main bathrooms) so their organization needs to be carefully considered. Designers' creativity brings together practical and esthetic aspects, offering solutions, which can be applied to all bathrooms. The furniture tends to be water-resist-ant, while accessories are useful elements which allow things to be organized in a simple way. Cupboards beneath sinks have doors and drawers for objects of personal hygiene and other accessories. Shelves can display decorative elements such as soaps and bath salts, or can serve to store sets of towels. Organizing a bathroom in an effective way is practical, but does not mean the esthetic aspect is forgotten. The following pages present examples of small and large bathrooms of different styles, with useful and clever solutions to always maintain order in this space.

Architect: **Unknown** *Location:* **Denmark** *Photography:* © K. Krogh / House of Pictures / Inside / Cover

Some simple shelves and drawers provide space for towels and personal hygiene products.

Architect: : **Alfons Soldevila** *Location:* **Alella, Spain** *Photography:* © **Jordi Miralles**

Interior design: **Michel Penneman** *Location:* Brussels, Belgium
Photography: © S. Anton / Inside / Cover

A complete walk-in wardrobe can be reached through an open bathroom, without being the same room.

■ *Architect:* Andy Macdonald *Location:* **Sydney, Australia** *Photography:* © Tom Ferguson

Making the most of the high ceiling, a small additional piece of furniture next to the sink makes more room.

The space beneath the sink is ideal for storage. Custom furniture makes the most of every last centimetre.

Architect: James Slade *Location:* New York, N.Y., U.S. *Photography:* © Jordi Miralles

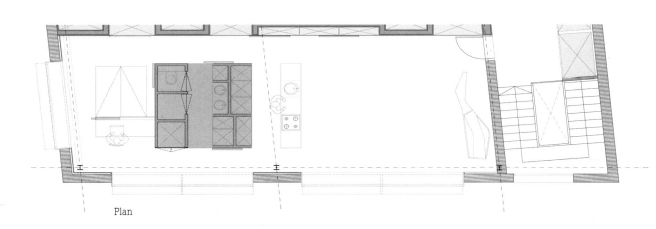

Plan

A passage connecting two rooms becomes more useful when you include a closet.

Architect: Cristina Fernández, Ignasi Pérez Arnal / Labb Arquitectura
Location: Granollers, Spain *Photography:* © Gogortza & Llorella

Architect: J. Gironés *Location:* Spain *Photography:* © Jordi Miralles

Accent colors and display shelves carved in the walls can turn a dull, narrow hallway {above, right} into a lively, interesting space.

Company: **Duravit** *Photography:* © Duravit

Small, light, freestanding or wall-hung: These are some of the options available to furnish a difficult space such as a bathroom.

Furniture & Accessories Design

Company: MB Studio Photography. © MB Studio

■ ■ *Company:* Duravit *Photography:* © Duravit

Bedrooms

SLEEP BETTER: ideas for more dream space

The bedroom is a place for rest, where a good sleep prepares us for the following day. These rooms often contain the bed, cupboards, bedside tables, dressers, and other elements that help organize our wardrobe, shoes, books, and other personal items. The design of bedroom furniture is highly evolved and the internal organization of each piece can be personalized according to the client's tastes. The materials used bestow character, such as lightness or richness, on a room and can unify spaces. In large houses, it is also possible to install dressing rooms or walk-in closets that afford us a lot more organizational space. Children's bedrooms often also function as studies and games rooms, so their furniture should be versatile, and the design must be age-appropriate. Colors play a crucial role here. In small homes, such as studios and lofts, the bedroom may share its space with other rooms and be situated on a mezzanine above the kitchen or the living room. It may even be hidden behind a piece of furniture or a simple sliding panel. Cupboards and chests of drawers in such cases can be transformed into multipurpose units. Their design, of course, should match the rest of the elements in the room. Another frequent solution is to combine the bedroom and the office in one space, which requires a layout and furniture that are compatible for both.

The wardrobe, made up of various modules, is located beneath the bed. A way of gaining space is to lift the bed and make the most of this space for the wardrobe, study, etc.

Architect: **Unknown** *Location:* **Madrid, Spain**
Photography: © **Luis Hevia**

Architect: Lucas Díaz *Location:* A Coruña, Spain *Photography:* © Luis Hevia

The headboard wall seems to be a reflection of the richly patterned hardwood floor. These contrast with the stark white wall containing the closet.

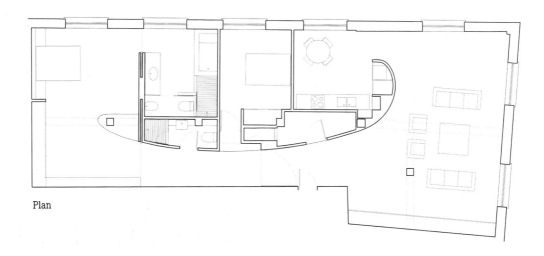

Plan

Architect: José Luis Maroto / Maroto e Ibáñez Arquitectos
Location: **Madrid, Spain** *Photography:* © Luis Hevia

The white color and the design without handles lets the wardrobes disappear into the background.

▌▌▐ The sleek built-in drawers wrap around the rough concrete column and beam above, while the hardwood floor adds a warm touch.

■■ *Architect:* AJS Designs *Location:* New York, N.Y., U.S. *Photography:* © Björg Magnea

This full-height built-in cabinet replaces freestanding dressers and fills an odd corner, giving the room a more harmonious shape.

The composition of one tall volume next to a long horizontal one is unified by an LED light strip at the base.

Architect: Hofman Dujardin Architecten *Location:* Amsterdam, the Netherlands
Photography: © Matthijs van Roon

Architect: Cho Slade *Location:* New York, N.Y., U.S. *Photography:* © Jordi Miralles

The bookshelf height reinforces the fact that two perpendicular walls of different heights are intersecting.

Architect: Joâo Pardal Monteiro *Location:* Lisboa, Portugal *Photography:* © FG+SG Fotografía de Arquitectura

The rail for a sliding ladder is nicely integrated into the design of the full-height closet while dividing it into upper and lower storage blocks. The sliding ladder makes it possible to reach the top of the closet.

Architect: José Manuel Álvarez *Location:* Oviedo, Spain *Photography:* © Luis Hevia

A platform on casters tucked under the bed provides easy-access storage space but is also a resourceful way to fit in a guest bed. The desk, also on casters, contributes to the flexible character of the room.

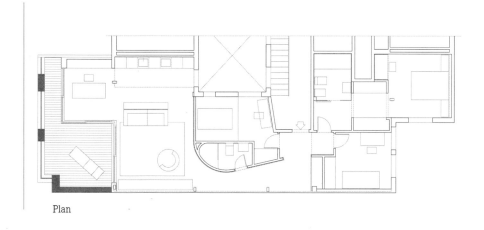

Plan

The bookshelves framing the bed are a contrasting element, emphasizing the presence of the mobile components.

The terms *storage* and *container* share the same concept. Above, the bedroom is contained within the limits set by the low walls.

Architect: Roger Bellera *Location:* Spain *Photography.* © Jordi Miralles

Architect: Joan Forgas *Location:* Taradell, Spain *Photography:* © Jordi Miralles

The horizontal niche above the bed creates a dynamic but clean and subtle detail that also serves to display some very special decorative elements.

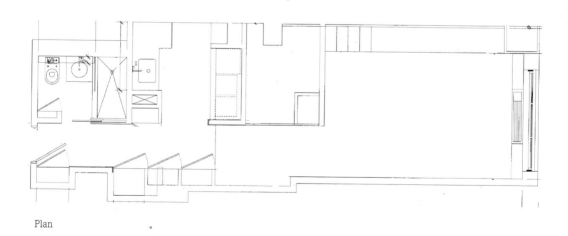

Plan

Taking advantage of the high ceiling, a bed platform provides generous space for storage underneath.

Architect: Kar-Hwa Ho *Location:* New York, N.Y., U.S. *Photography:* © Björg Magnea

Architect: Page Goolrick *Location:* New York, N.Y., U.S. *Photography:* © John M. Hall

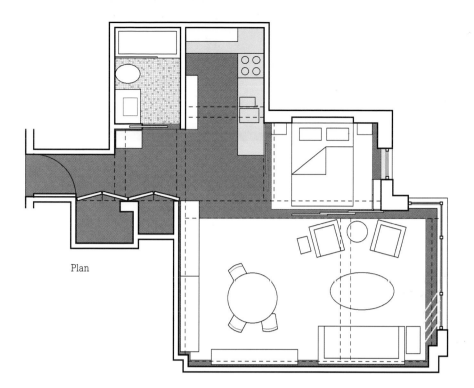

Plan

In this open-plan apartment, light moving panels close off the bedroom for added privacy. The platform storage bed converts the wasted space under the bed into a convenient container.

Architect: Manel Torres/ IN Decoración *Location:* Palau de Plegamans, Spain *Photography:* © José Luis Hausmann

Ready-made closets provide a wide variety of ways to organize personal belongings, using combinations of different-size modules and finishes to adapt easily to the space.

Architect: Fernando Muñoz Gómez *Location:* Madrid, Spain *Photography:* © Luis Hevia

Store-bought furniture and accessories can allow us to organize a space without building walls. The result is often a fun and clever solution for anyone on a tight budget.

Clean lines and planes characterize this project, where storage disappears behind surfaces. | *Interior design:* **Francesc Rifé** *Location:* **Barcelona, Spain** *Photography:* © **Gogortza & Llorella**

Architect: Jordi Queralt *Location:* **Barcelona, Spain** *Photography:* © Jordi Miralles

Small containers stacked on open shelves express order and discipline even more than conventional closets.

Interior design: **Alicia Magañá** *Location:* **Vallromanes, Spain** *Photography:* © José Luis Hausmann

Besides serving their original purpose, small containers and accessories quickly personalize a room.

Architect: Unknown *Location:* Denmark *Photography:* © L. Wendendahl / House of Pictures / Inside / Cover

Wall-hung bookshelves are meant to clear up floor area, but it is tempting to stack old magazines, boxes, and shoes under them.

Architect: Unknown *Location:* Madrid, Spain *Photography:* © Luis Hevia

A low bookshelf fills in the gap between the wall and the column of rough-sawn wood. It provides a physical separation between the sitting area and the bed without obstructing the view.

The bed slides under the book shelf, thus the living room is easily converted into a bedroom.

Architect: AvroKO *Location:* New York, N.Y., U.S. *Photography:* © Gogortza & Llorella

A Murphy bed is the ultimate solution when it comes to making the most of a small space.

When lowered, a Murphy bed often reveals lateral space, perfect for an integrated reading light and bookshelves.

Architect: Daylin Torres / Cru 2001 Location: Barcelona, Spain Photography: © Gogortza & Llorella

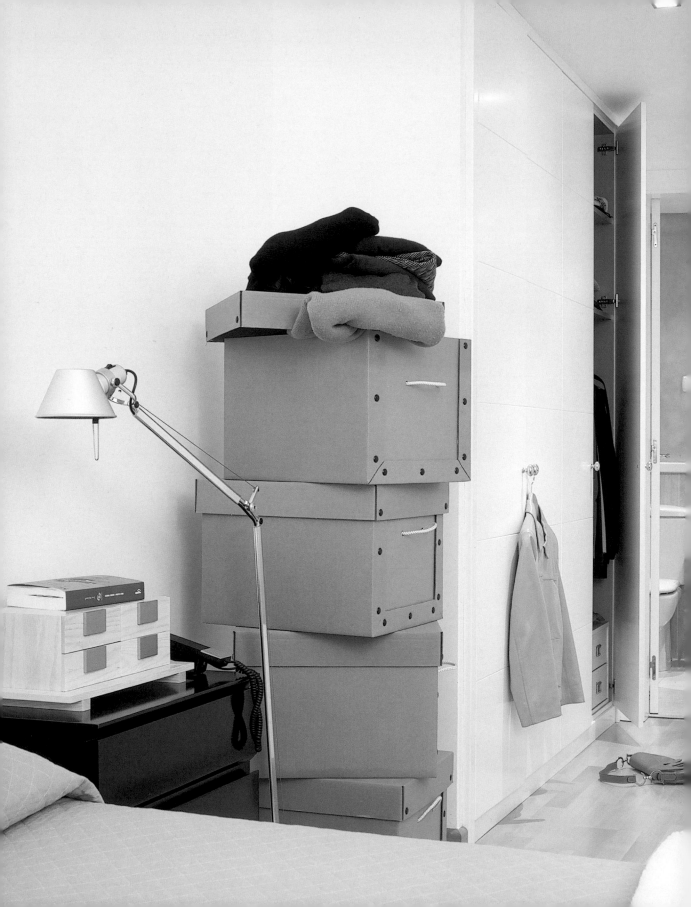

A pile of boxes, whether metal or cardboard, can become a sculptural storage tower.

Architect: Oriol Moyà *Location:* Spain *Photography:* © Jordi Miralles

Company: Zanotta *Photography:* © Zanotta

Furniture & Accessories Design

Company: **MB Studio** *Photography:* © **MB Studio** | Model of a closet with aluminum structure. Dapasso doors made of transparent glass with rail inthe ceiling.

Following lifestyle trends, designers are focusing on creating durable, easy-to-maintain bedroom furniture that is based on simple shapes, with little or no ornamentation.

Closet with smoked glass shelves. Gray oak drawer.

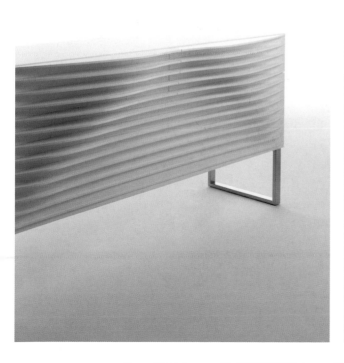

Above. Night dresser with SLIMDRAWER drawer. MB Studio.
Below. TIDE chest of drawers, by Karim Rashid for Horm.

below images | *Company:* **Horm** *Photography:* © **Karim Rashid**

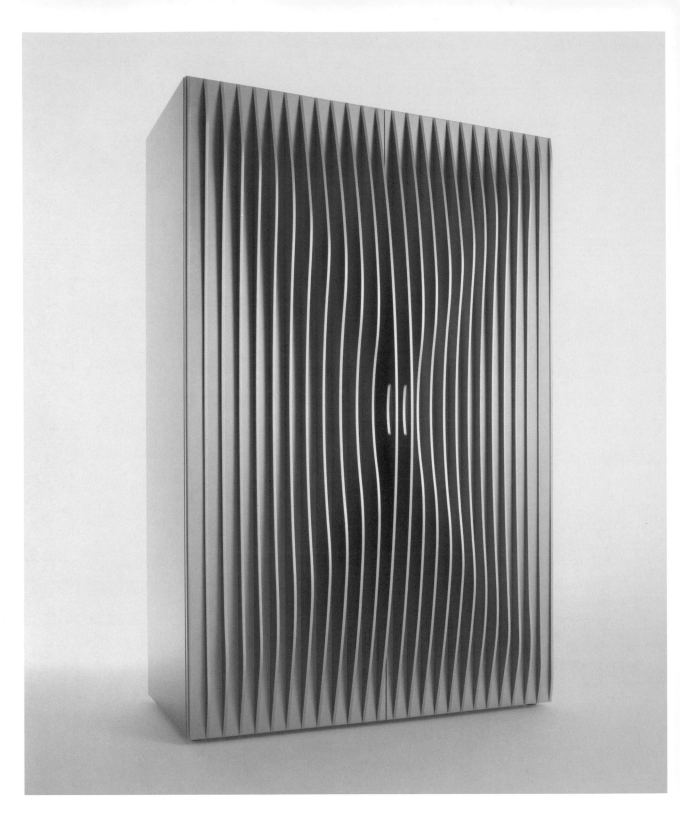

BLEND wardrobe. Design by Karim Rashid for Horm. Although function usually follows shape, technology has allowed us to make interesting use of materials and forms that were unimaginable not so long ago.

WOGG 21 wardrobe. Design Benny Mosimann.

Company: Wogg *Photography:* © Wogg

Home Offices

WORK BETTER: ways to have room to think

The office is one of the rooms in the house that requires the most order. The use of the Internet has extended to many homes in recent years, and they often have spaces designed especially to accommodate a computer. Both in small rooms and in larger rooms, office space is gaining in importance within the home. For people who are self-employed and need offices in order to work from home, these spaces take on more importance and are often located in larger, well-lit rooms. Small offices are often in smaller rooms or in corners of other rooms such as a living room or bedroom. In some cases, it is necessary to install a divider to separate the two spaces. In any case, the organization of the space and the storage must be adjusted to the type of objects kept there. The most commonly used elements are desks, shelves, modular furniture or bookcases to hold books, folders, boxes, and files of all types. Drawers are situated beneath work tables and can be used to store objects used at the desk. Many of these pieces of furniture are on casters, which makes the layout of the study more flexible, allowing it to quickly change according to the needs of the user. The decoration of the space and choice of furniture determine the final look and style of the room.

Architect: Simon Eisinger *Location:* New York, N.Y., U.S. *Photography:* © Gogortza & Llorella

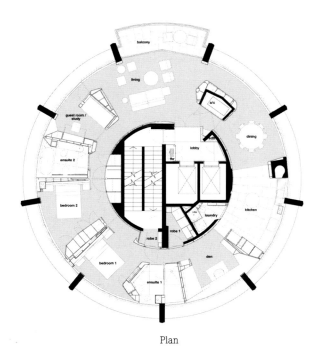

Plan

Architect: **Stanic Harding** *Location:* **Sydney, Australia** *Photography:* © Paul Gosney

Fold-out desks cover two functions: In the closed position, as containers, and in the open position as work surfaces.

Architect: Unknown *Location:* Barcelona, Spain *Photography:* © Gogortza & Llorella

Filing cabinets and the glass surface make up the table. The drawers are used for office materials.

The mezzanine has been extended along the wall to accommodate a floor-to-ceiling bookshelf.

Architect. Manuel Salgado *Location:* Lisboa, Portugal *Photography:* © FG+SG Fotografía de Arquitectura

Architect: João Pardal Monteiro *Location:* Lisboa, Portugal *Photography:* © FG+SG Fotografía de Arquitectura

When the panel slides to the right it divides the sitting room and the entry hall. When it slides to the left, it covers the office bookshelf and opens up the space.

A small office can be placed in any corner. The book shelf separates it from the other rooms.

Interior design: Owners *Location:* **Unknown** *Photography:* © W. Heath / H&L / Inside / COVER

Architect: Unknown *Location:* Madrid, Spain *Photography:* © Luis Hevia

A bookcase on casters separates the office from the sitting area and is useful to both areas.

Architect: Silvia Via *Location:* Barcelona, Spain *Photography:* © Gogortza & Llorella

A partition separating functional areas is also used for work stations and overhead shelves. The walls are lined with built-in shelves.

Interior design: Toby Orford *Location:* Cape Town, South Africa *Photography:* © K. Bernstein / H&L / Inside / COVER

The white shelves, both built-in and freestanding, seem to blend with the space that contains them; only the items really make them visible.

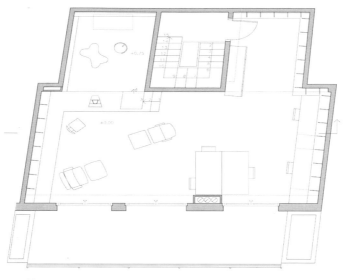

Plan

Architect: **Agustí Costa** *Location:* **Berga, Spain**
Photography: © David Cardelús

Inspired by the iconic Charles Eames chair and ottoman, sleek black painted surfaces combined with oak shelving to create a calm environment. The cantilevered wooden step leads to an adjacent room.

Architect: José Manuel Álvarez *Location:* Oviedo, Spain *Photography:* © Luis Hevia

The light metal shelving and the glass tabletop contrast with the heavy trestles. The long glass door reinforces this contrast.

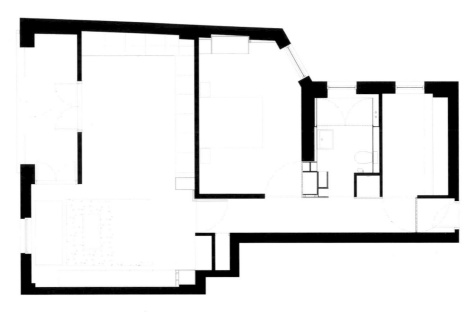

Plan

Architect: **Andy Macdonald** *Location:* **Sydney, Australia** *Photography:* © Tom Ferguson

A fold-down table provides an additional work surface in a room where space is limited.

Interior design: Francesc Rifé Location: Barcelona, Spain Photography: © Gogortza & Llorella

A small space in the study is arranged as a living room, which is used for meetings and moments of rest.

Interior design: Francesc Rifé *Location:* Barcelona, Spain *Photography:* © Eugeni Pons

A dark, heavily articulated built-in bookcase contrasts with the stark white interior. The result is a very modern environment. Recessed and overhead lighting also play an important role in creating this effect.

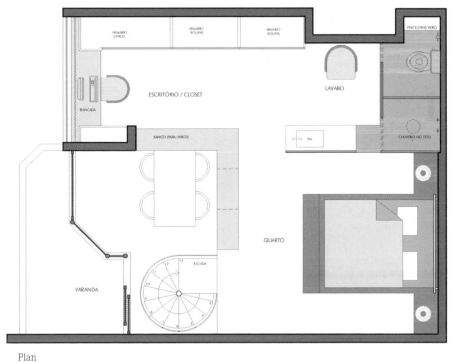

Plan

The study is located on the first floor and in the same space as the bedroom, dressing room and a small bathroom.

Architect: Fernandes Capanema Arquitetura *Location:* Brasilia, Brazil *Photography:* © Marri Nogueira, Clausem Bonifacio

The mirrors of the wardrobe visually enlarge the space. The chosen furniture and its arrangement make for a unified décor which adapts to the room's different uses.

WOGG 22 model Slim Shelf System.

Furniture & Accessories Design

WOGG 18 Model Sideboard. Designed by Benny Mosimann

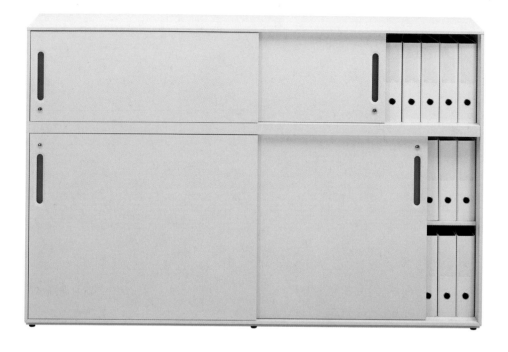

Company: Vitra *Photography:* © Marc Eggimann / Vitra

ACSU Model, by Antonio Citterio for Vitra. Filing cabinets and the glass surface make up the table. The drawers are used for office materials.

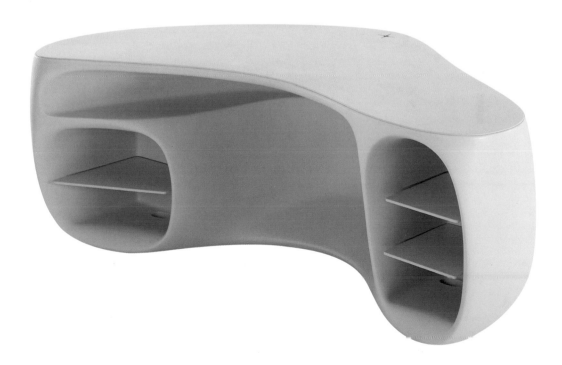

BOBAB Model, by Philippe Starck for Vitra. The use of plastic has allowed more flexibility in office furniture design. The ease of manufacturing helps simplify design and packaging but, most important, assembly by the user.

CAVOUR table, by Carlo Mollino, 1949. Some pieces of furniture are design classics that manage to be contemporary.

Above. CAVOUR table, by Carlo Mollino, 1949. Below. COMACINA table. Design from 1930 by Piero Bottoni.
More conventional materials, such as wood, metal and glass, are still mainly used in office furniture thanks to their strength and durability.

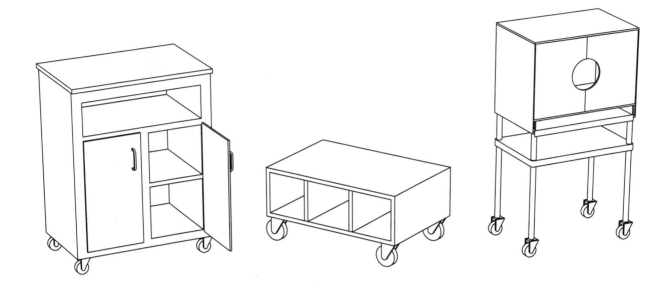

Company: **Kabalab** *Photography:* © Kabalab

Model by KABAFURNITURE. Bin for small office.
Filing cabinets and the glass surface make up the table. The drawers are used for office materials.

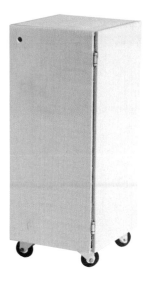

CARUSO model. Folding desk.

Living Rooms

previous page | *Architect:* **Kar-Hwa Ho** *Location:* **New York, N.Y., U.S.** *Photography:* © Björg Magnea

RELAX BETTER: solutions to help you unwind

The living room is the house's main meeting room, the center of social and family life. This is where relatives and friends gather and where long and pleasant chats take place. The layout of this space depends on the room's dimensions and its relationship to other rooms in the home. The living room is often connected to the dining room, and on some occasions it can be found next to the kitchen. In lofts or apartments with only one room, it is usually the furniture and its distribution that defines a space. The living room can usually be identified by the presence of sofas, bookshelves, coffee tables, and pieces that hold televisions and audio equipment. The furniture where personal objects can be stored defines the character of the occupants. Bookcases tend to hold decorative objects, as well as books that have been collected over the years. More books and magazines can be found on the coffee tables. The design solutions presented by architects, interior designers, and even owners for this room aim to provide space without making a particular decorative and personal style stand out. Thus, if a space is small, choosing a tall bookshelf or a coffee table with storage room will add space to this area. If the living room is larger it can be furnished with medium-height pieces of furniture that will add a sense of spaciousness.

Architect: Agustí Costa *Location:* Vilada, Spain *Photography:* © David Cardelús

Without interfering with the original aesthetic of the space, the frosted-glass bookshelf is used as a glowing divider filtering the light and bringing a touch of modernity into the space.

Architect: Ares Fernández Location: Barcelona, Spain Photography: © José Luis Hausmann

A cabinet and several shelves have been cut into the wall as part of the fireplace surround composition.

A simple bench beneath the window creates space for the music system and some decorative objects. ▪▐▐▐

■|■ *Architect:* Agustí Costa *Location:* Berga, Spain *Photography:* © David Cardelús

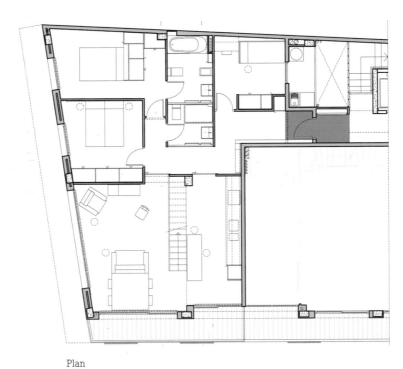

Plan

The stair is the central component of the design, acting as the divider between the living room and the kitchen. The solid-wood guardrail extends to the floor to enclose the space underneath the stair, which is used for storage.

The back wall of this sitting area is made interesting by incorporating a Cartesian grid, finished to match the wall.

Architect: Eduard Samso *Location:* Barcelona, Spain *Photography:* © Jordi Miralles

Architect: Alberto Marcos *Location:* Madrid, Spain *Photography:* © Luis Hevia

This interesting wood-clad back wall features a number of foldaway shelves forming a grid. ▮▮▮

An original plastic curtain surrounds the bath structure, creating a private area.

Architect: **Feyferlik-Fritzer** *Location:* Vienna, Austria *Photography:* © Paul Ott, Graz

The whole length of one wall is used as support for open shelves, combining well with the solid-wood elements on the opposite walls.

The bookcase's metal structure creates empty spaces which make the piece seem lighter, while also providing a useful space.

Architect: Inés Rodríguez / Air Projects *Location:* Barcelona, Spain
Photography: © Jordi Miralles

The custom-made cupboards make room for storage, while the color white lets them blend into the space.

A collection of miniature chairs is displayed on a striking bookcase, which also separates the study area from the dining room.

Architect: Raul Campderich / Air Projects Location: Barcelona, Spain Photography: © Jordi Miralles

Architect: Lagranja *Location:* Sant Cugat, Spain *Photography:* © Luis Hevia

Shelves full of books are lined up against the walls, framing the glass door. The music system and radiators are hidden beneath a wooden step.

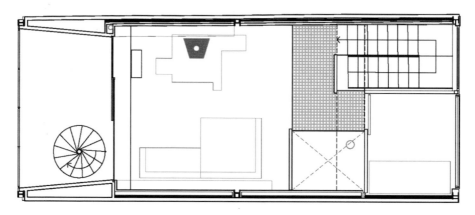

Plan

Bookshelves on casters can easily be wheeled wherever needed, against a wall or as a divider between two spaces.

Architect: **Unknown** *Location:* **Madrid, Spain** *Photography:* © **Luis Hevia**

The different types of shelves (modular, for CDs or pieces of art) create a dynamic and youthful space.

Architect: Rocío Fueyo *Location:* Madrid, Spain *Photography:* © Jordi Miralles

The small pieces of furniture match to create a personal decoration. Pictures and photographs are placed on a shelf above the sofa. CD towers are placed next to a bright piece of furniture in the entrance hall.

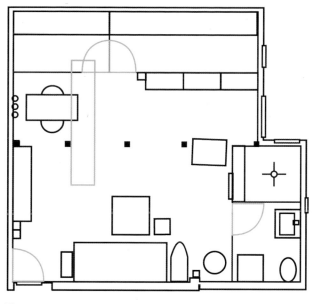

Plan

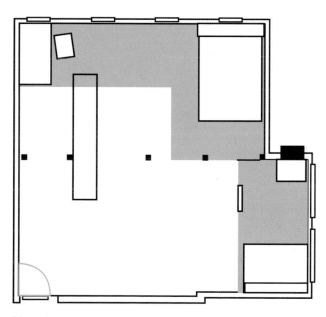

Mezzanine

The interior volume of the space is unobstructed and free of any large element. ▮▮

Architect: Javier Hernández Mingo *Location:* Madrid, Spain *Photography:* © Luis Hevia

Generous storage spaces are a luxury. When the rooms used on a daily basis are stripped of unnecessary possessions, a home becomes a refuge from the chaotic and cluttered environment outside.

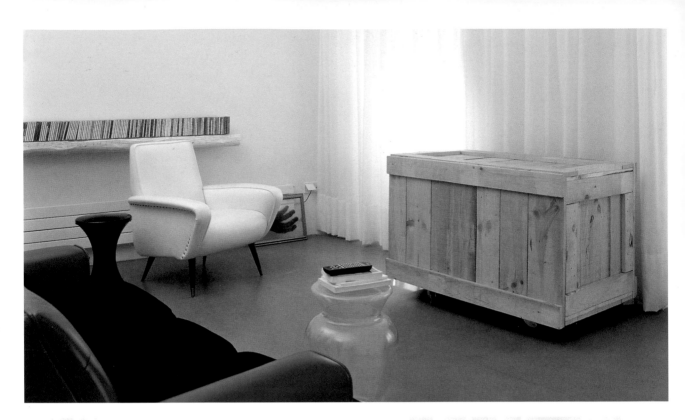

Found objects taken out of their original context can become clever solutions with little effort.

The combination of doors and drawers with open shelves makes room for all kinds of objects.

Architect: AJS Designs *Location:* New York, N.Y., U.S. *Photography:* © Björg Magnea

Architect: Unknown *Location:* Madrid, Spain *Photography:* © Luis Hevia

Concentrating multiple functions in one piece of storage cabinetry along the wall frees up floor surface. The challenge is to organize the spaces and the functions contained in this one section in the most efficient possible way.

Architect: Stefano Colli Location: Barcelona, Spain Photography: © José Luis Hausmann

The study and dining room share the same space. A simple piece of furniture with drawers can be confused with the shelves.

The bookshelf has a mobile module which slides on rails, to provide additional space.

Architect: Fernandes Capanema Arquitetura *Location:* Brasilia, Brazil *Photography:* © Marri Nogueira, Clausem Bonifacio

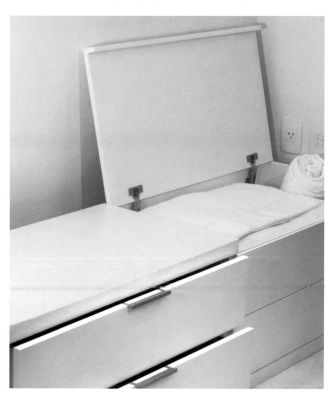

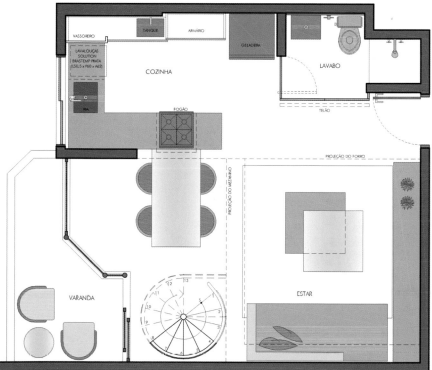

Plan

Made to fit against the wall, this long and low cabinet is accessed both from the front and the top to maximize its use. ◼▮▮

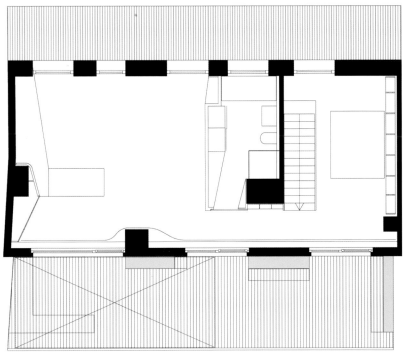

Plan

Architect: ARTEC Architekten *Location:* Vienna, Austria *Photography:* © Marc Lins

Odd corners that can't be used in any other way can always accommodate more shelves.

This personal design makes the most of the space beneath the seats and next to the window where cupboards and drawers are installed.

Take advantage of any opportunity to make the most of space. The idea is to think of any unused corner as an opportunity to incorporat drawers, pull-out cabinets, or fold-up surfaces.

Architect: Morq *Location:* Rome, Italy *Photography:* © Morq

This clever use of movable panels in front of a wall with shelves makes an always changing and dynamic space, exposing or revealing different sections of the wall behind.

Architect: Alberto Caetano *Location:* Lisboa, Portugal *Photography:* © FG+SG Fotografía de Arquitectura

A generous, high ceiling can be an opportunity for vertical storage with a small footprint. The lower, more accessible section could serve everyday functions, while the upper section could hold items only used occasionally.

■■■ *Company:* Rafemar *Photography:* © Rafemar

Furniture & Accessories Design

The BLOCS model is made of three basic elements which can be combined and adapted to the available space in every home.

Above. DOOR model, book shelf with individual doors.
Below. PAM BUFETTE model with lots of space.

PAM BAR. High sideboard with mirror, light, inner shelves and an extendable tray.

Company: **Rafemar** Photography: © **Rafemar** | The PAM shelf is made with oak, cherry and ebony wood. The finishes can also be lacquered or of wengué wood.

BLOCS model with lacquered finish. The modules can also be placed vertically.

Company: *Lago* Photography: © Lago | 36E8 System. Design Daniele Lago.

Bright colors and geometric shapes work well together. They can form an eye-catching element or a central piece of furniture in a space.

Company: Kabalab *Photography:* © Kabalab | KABAFURNITURE armchair and sofa

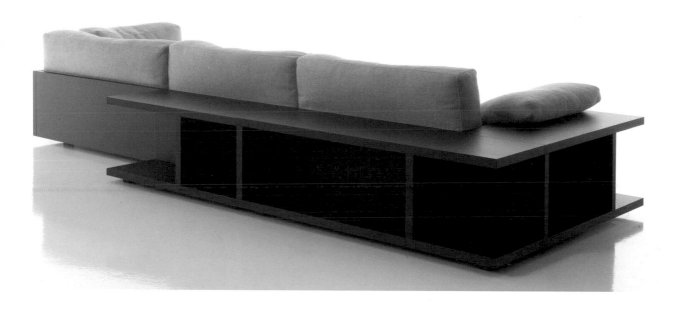

MEX bookshelf and sofa, designed by Piero Lissoni. | *Company:* Cassina *Photography.* © Cassina

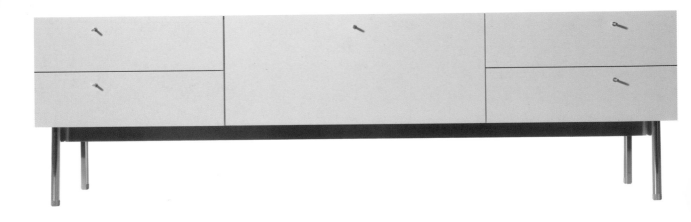

Company: **Cassina** *Photography:* © **Cassina** | FLAT model, designed by Piero Lissoni.

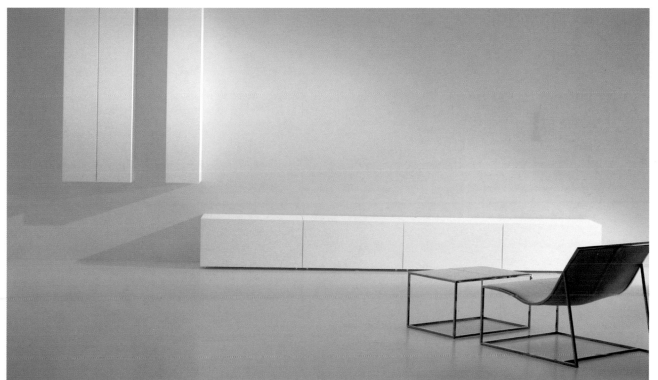

DO IT collection, designed by VCCB. | *Company.* Viccarbe *Photography:* © Viccarbe

Company: Mb Studio Photography: © Mb Studio | Stackable bins by WALLBOX with folding doors. "Bucs" with SLIMDRAWER drawers. Designed by Marino Rossato.

Thanks to the use of durable, low-maintenance materials that are also attractive, furniture design has evolved to produce more functional and comfortable pieces.

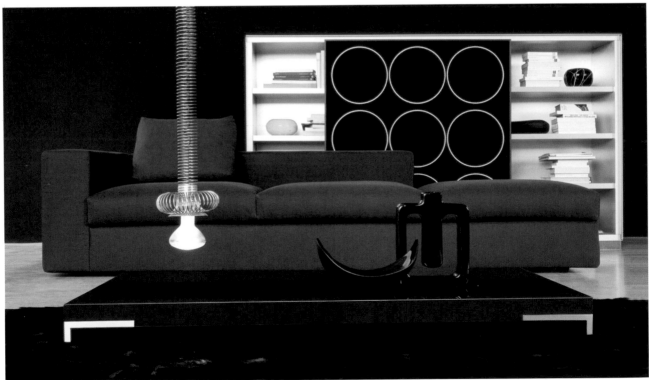

Above. SOHO table. Designed by Emaf Progetti.
Below. SPEED shelf with sliding door. Designed by Carlo Colombo.

The SLIM shelf behind the sofa has diagonal separators. Designed by Todd Bracher.

Eames Storage Unit (ESU), designed by Charles & Ray Eames, 1949.
ESU units were one of the first modular designs made of standardized parts.

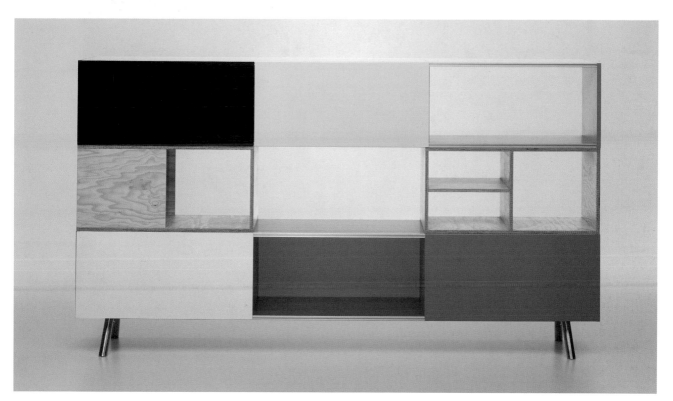

KAST Bookcase, designed by Maarten Van Severen. The designs have a pleasant minimalist look, reinforced by simple plywood and steel components, as well as painted panels.

Company: Vitra *Photography:* © Marc Eggimann / Vitra

Company: **MDF** *Photography:* © MDF

Above. BOX model. Designed by James Irvine.
Below. RANDOM shelf. Designed by Neuland Industriedesign.

The RANDOM bookshelf is made of wooden panels of medium thickness, painted in white. The openings are distributed following standard measurements. They can be attached to the wall and have adjustable legs.

Stairs & Hallways

Previous page | *Architect:* Alberto Marcos *Location:* Madrid, Spain *Photography:* © Luis Hevia

ORGANIZE BETTER: ways to use forgotten spaces

Passageways, stairs, hallways, corridors: All these areas can be used for storage. Wall-hugging shelving, bookcases, or cupboards in these narrow spaces afford more storage without overloading other rooms. These zones can be used to store everyday belongings or those that are not used on a daily basis. They are ideal, for example, for keeping clothing, linens, or objects of sentimental value that we do not want to dispose of. These areas can house ironing boards, cleaning products, or books that no longer fit in the living room or office. Of course, the potential of these spaces will depend on the layout of the home, though solutions can always be found even in smaller homes, with a little creativity. For example, a chest of drawers, which holds more than a bookcase, would fit in a hall. The integration of stairway and hallway furniture into the decor of a home can be done in different ways. One option is to visually integrate the cupboards in a hall or stairway with the rest of the house by employing the same materials and using simple hardware that doesn't attract attention. That way, such areas are not overloaded and maintain visual continuity. Another option is to choose furniture that does stand out, thus creating contrasts and lending dynamism to the home's aesthetics. These solutions can be applied to any home, regardless of the available surface area.

The wardrobes have been placed in the space between the bedroom and the bathroom, creating a walk-in closet. | *Architect.* José Manuel Álvarez *Location.* Oviedo, Spain *Photography.* © Luis Hevia

The spaciousness of some corridors can be used for cupboards and other storage elements.

Architect: Unknown Location: Barcelona, Spain Photography: © Gogortza & Llorella

Storage options are endless for halls and staircases. Pieces can either be custom-built for better integration into an existing space or ready-made to fulfill the need to store various items.

Custom closets can be made with the combination of drawers, shelves, etc. provided by the manufacturers.

Architect: Carlos Cruz, Pedro Alarçao *Location:* Porto, Portugal *Photography:* © FG+SG Fotografía do Arquitectura

The doors and handles are so discrete here that they blend in seamlessly with the style and palette of the hallway.

Architect: ARTEC Architekten Location: Vienna, Austria Photography: © Marc Lins

Wardrobes near the stairs provide more storage space. The kitchen is integrated into this area.

The design for some needed shelves is incorporated into a wall on one side of the stairs. Also, the area under the stairs allows for additional storage.

Architect: Carlos Castanheira *Location:* Porto, Portugal *Photography:* © FG+SG Fotografía de Arquitectura

Conceived to make the most of a small space, the stairway is an extension of a sculptural rank of cupboards. Together, these elements incorporate the architectural ethos of the home and fulfill the need for storage.

An architectural feature that is intended for storage, also serves, in this case, as a spatial divider.

Architect: Alberto Caetano *Location:* Estoril, Portugal *Photography:* © FG+SG Fotografía de Arquitectura

■▮▮▮ *Architect:* Unknown *Location:* Unknown *Photography:* © W. Heath / H&L / Inside / Cover

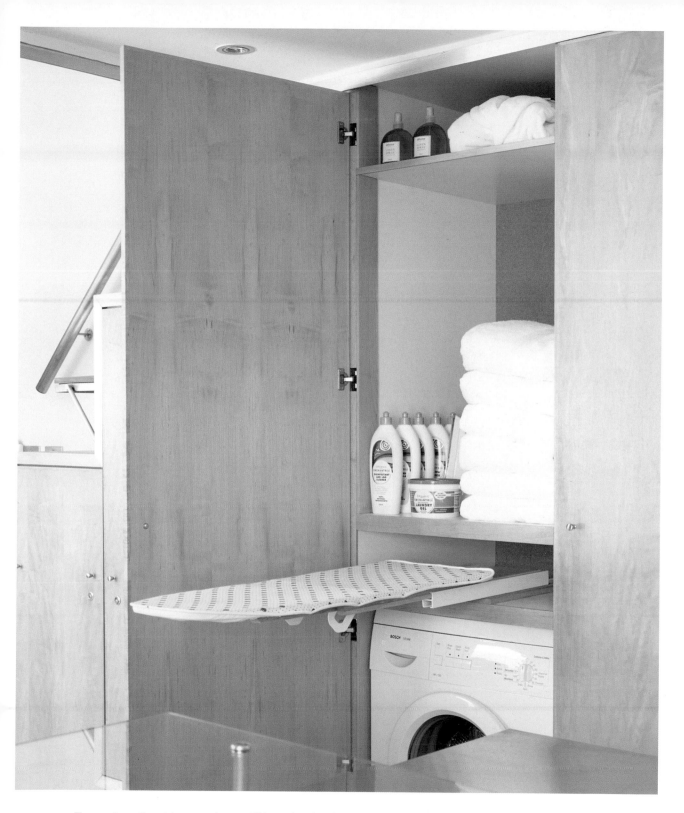

The area beneath a stairway can house utilities such as laundry rooms, wine cellars, and closets. All this is concealed behind panels and doors completely integrated into the design of the stairs.

Architect: Paulo David *Location:* Madeira, Portugal *Photography:* © FG+SG Fotografía de Arquitectura

The door to one room, here a bathroom, can also lead into a built-in closet, thereby simplifying the design.

Plan

Architect: M2 Arquitectura *Location:* Sabadell, Spain *Photography:* © José Hevia

Overhead storage was built above the walkway, defined by the long, narrow entry mat.

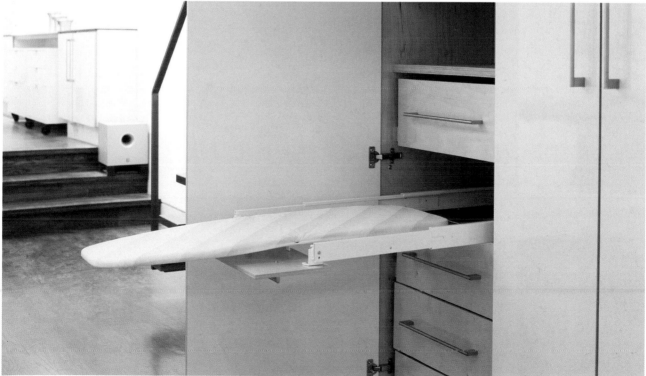

Cupboards beneath the stairs are for a variety of objects, including a bicycle or an ironing board.

Architect: AvroKO *Location:* New York, N.Y., U.S. *Photography:* © Cogortza & Llorella

Architect: Andrade Morettin *Location:* Sao Paulo, Brasil *Photography:* © Nelson Kon

These shelves hang from a track and, when moved, enable a constantly changing environment by separating or connecting spaces. ▮▮▮

Top image | *Architect:* **Ricardo Bak Gordon** *Location:* **Lisboa, Portugal**
Photography: © FG+SG Fotografía de Arquitectura

Above. The contrast between the bare wall and the white doors makes
the built-in wardrobe stand out.

The custom-built shelves are the main feature of this project. The corridor is separated from the room thanks to the sliding doors.

Architect: Joao Santa Rita *Location:* Lisboa, Portugal
Photography: © FG+SG Fotografía de Arquitectura

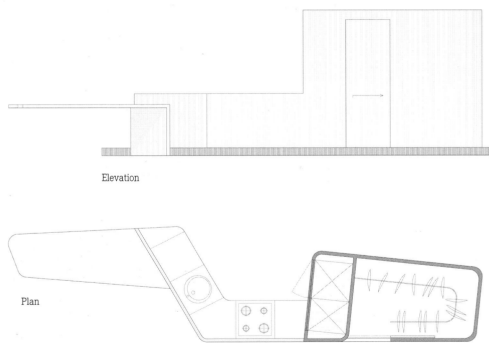

Elevation

Plan

Architect: Cristina Fernández, Ignasi Pérez Arnal / Labb Arquitectura *Location:* Barcelona, Spain *Photography:* © Gogortza & Llorella

An eye-catching volume in the middle of the loft includes the kitchen and a walk-in closet.

Architect: Cristina Fernández, Ignasi Pérez Arnal / Labb Arquitectura
Location: Granollers, Spain *Photography:* © Gogortza & Llorella

A built-in closet, painted in the same color as the walls, is placed between the bedroom and the bathroom.

The space around the supporting pillar is used for an additional wardrobe.

Architect: Stanic Harding *Location:* Sydney, Australia *Photography:* © Paul Gosney

Architect: João Pardal Monteiro Location: Lisboa, Portugal
Photography: © FG+SG Fotografía de Arquitectura

Above, an oval structure bisecting functional areas contains cabinets.

Company: Porro *Photography:* © Porro   STORAGE program of wardrobes. Design by Piero Lissoni + CRS.

Furniture & Accessories Design

STORAGE program of wardrobes and walk-in closets. Design by Piero Lissoni + CRS.

Built-in, custom designs are an expression of quality and durability. However, catalog storage modules allow us to choose the combination of elements best suited to our need. STORAGE program of wardrobes. Design by Piero Lissoni + CRS.

STORAGE program of wardrobes and walk-in closets. Design by Piero Lissoni + CRS.

■■■ *Company:* **Porro** *Photography:* © **Porro** | STORAGE program of wardrobes and walk-in closets. Design by Piero Lissoni + CRS.

Companies selling storage furniture help their costumers find the best finishes and configurations. They often help locate someone to assemble the pieces, too.

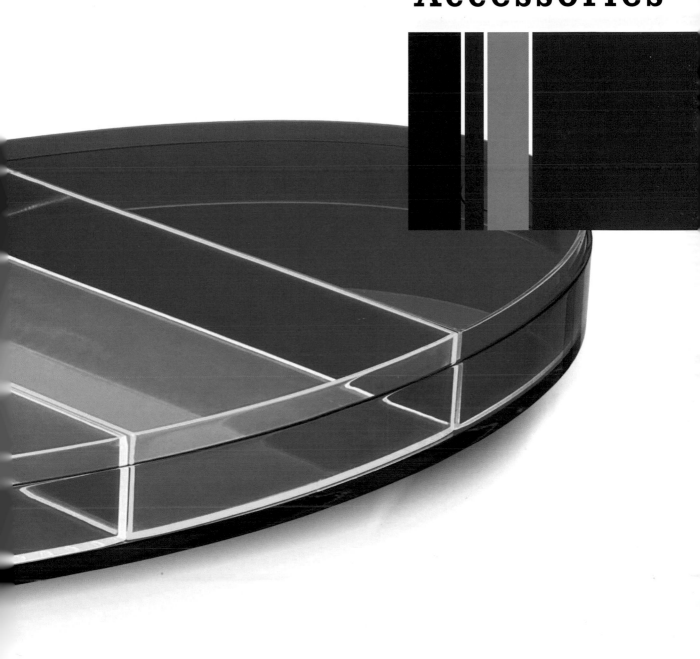

■■■ *Company:* **Sawaya & Moroni** *Photography:* © **Sawaya & Moroni** │ O'VALEO tray. Design by William Azuaya.

DESIGN BETTER: the solutions are in the details

■■■ The designs for storage accessories in the home have advanced in recent years from two points of view: the quality of the designs and materials, and the usefulness of the final product. Taking care when choosing materials, from traditional cardboard to plastics or recyclable materials, can help to create good quality products. Manufacturers are aware that a good design is an element that adds value to a product and in many cases have depended on a collaboration with well respected design teams. It must not be forgotten that a good object must carry out the functions it has been designed for and must be practical, helping to maintain order in the house. The products on display in the following pages are just a small representation of objects designed for the home to facilitate the storage of small items, from photos to contact lenses. There are small formats designs, like card holders, and other larger ones, like multipurpose containers. There is also a wide variety of boxes of different sizes and materials: metal, cardboard, wood, etc. Innovative ideas can also be found, such as an original soffit for storing many objects of different sizes. The styles of these different proposals can also be adapted to different tastes, although original designs with bright colors and daring shapes are more dominant. Finally, it is important to mention that there are both proposals from big, well-established brands, such as Vitra or Vinçon, as well as from young designers and smaller emerging companies.

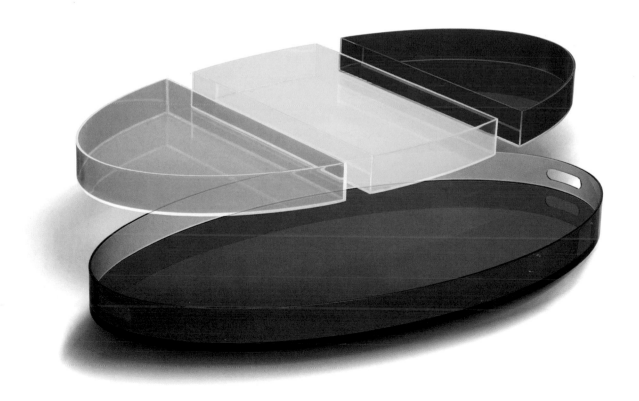

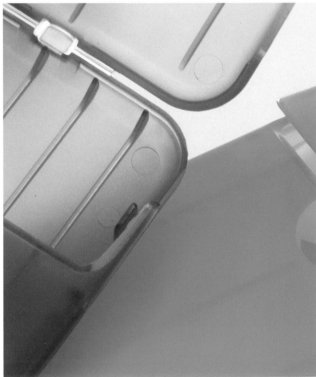

Company: Kabalab *Photography:* © Kabalab | KABACASE card holder.

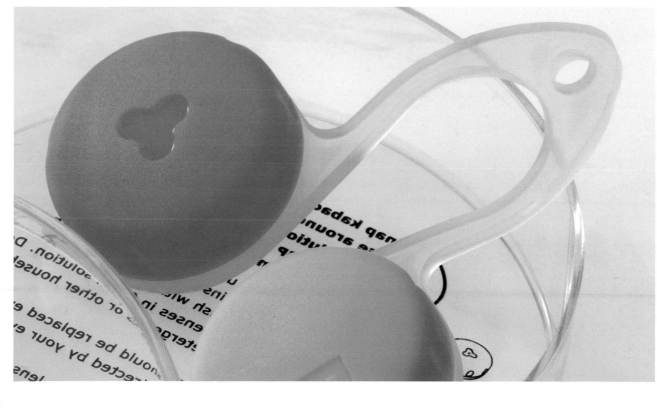

KABACLIP case for contact lenses. Vibrant colors can make small storage products more appealing.

Company: Wildwood Creations Inc. *Photography:* © Wildwood Creations Inc.

TOY BOXES. These colorful boxes in the shapes of friendly animals help children organize their toys in a fun way. ▮▮▮

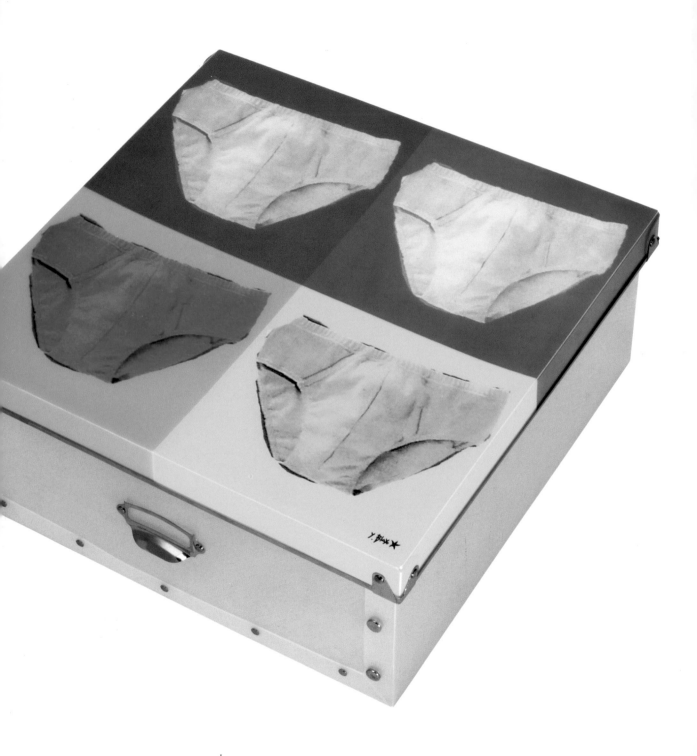

Above. CAJA CARTAS. Below. CAJA JARDÍN.
Boxes can be personalized in order to facilitate the search for items.

Company: Vinçon *Photography:* © Vinçon

ME BOX boxes. In the numbered boxes a grid of preperforated holes lets us create a personal coding system for boxes.

Different models of recycled cardboard boxes VINÇON.
Below right. Plastic stackable bins. ▮▮

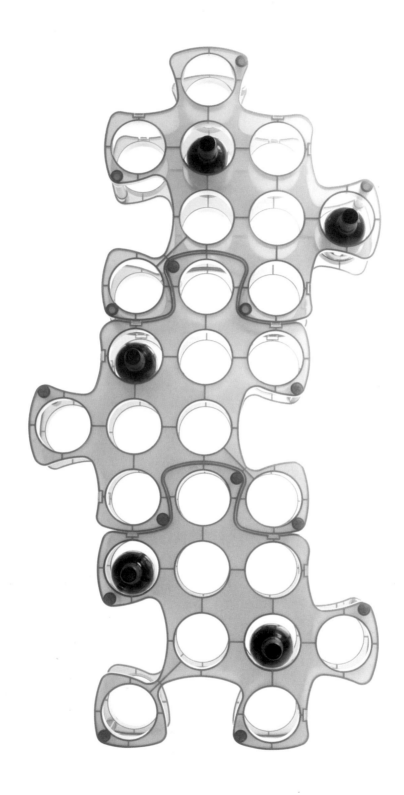

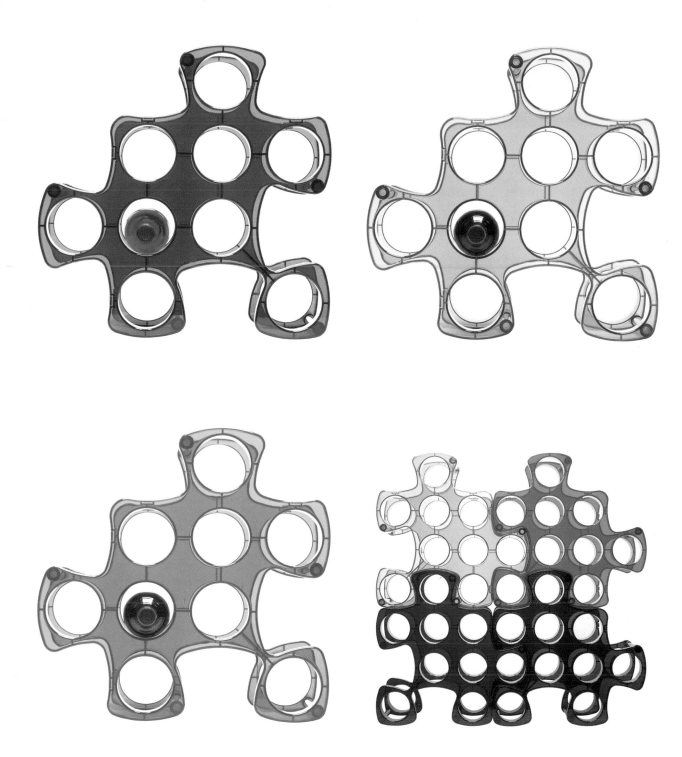

PUZZLE WINE RACK. The modules of the puzzle-shaped wine rack can be configured in multiple colors and shapes.

BOX model. Design by Ronan & Erwan Bouroullec.

Plafón UTEN SILO II. Design by Dorothee Becker. This very handy organizer can be attached to any vertical surface. ▌▏

Company: Massieoffice *Photography:* © Massieoffice

FLYING VEE book case. This simple right-angle element allows us to create our own composition. It can be used as a shelf or bookend.

Company: **Wogg** *Photography:* © Wogg

PILAR BOX bins. Design by Hans Eichenberger.
This colorful, utilitarian cylinder adapts to diverse uses. It is attractive enough for any room of the house.

| WOGG 12 Sideboard STRIPE bin. Design by Robert and Trix Haussmann. Collapsible low cabinets make a practical chest of drawers, and they make the moving experience less painful.

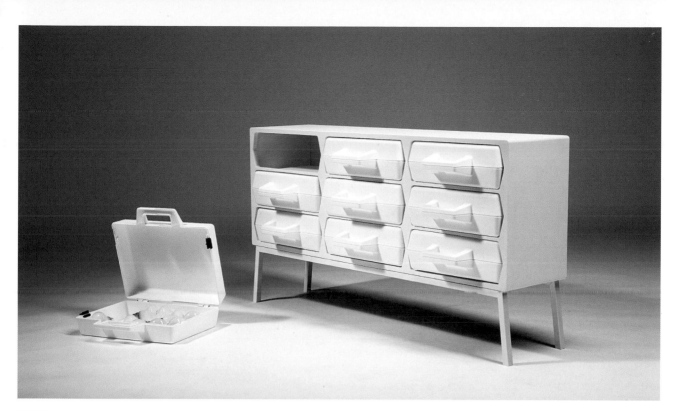

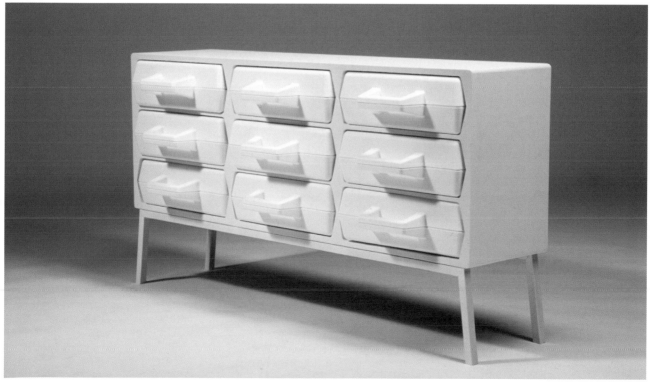

TAKE OUT model. Design by Klaus Aalto. | *Company:* **Imu Design** *Photography:* © Imu Design

Company: **Viable London** Photography: © **Viable London** | SHELF LIFE book shelf.

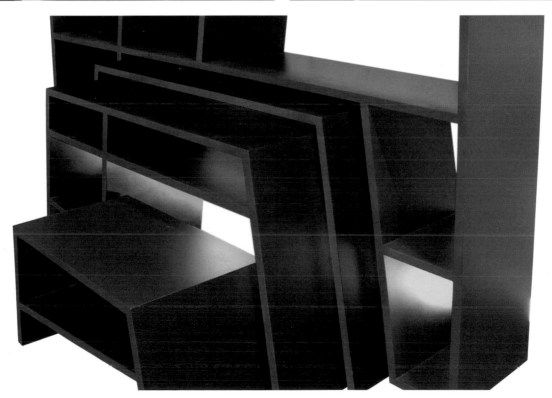

Above. SHELF LIFE book shelf. Below. SHELF LIFE DESK.
A chair and a desk come out of the bookcase when needed and can disappear again as part of the structure to clear up floor space.

BULTHAUP
Bulthaup GmbH & Co KG
Aich / Werkstraße 6
84155 Bodenkirchen, Germany
Ph. +49 8741 800
F. +49 8741 803 09
www.bulthaup.com

CASSINA
Cassina S.p.A.
Via Busnelli 1
20036 Meda, Italy
Ph. +39 0362 3721
F. +39 0362 3422 46
www.cassina.it

DAGAN DESIGN
Dagan Design Inc.
986 Vernon Ave.
90291 Venice CA, USA
Ph. +1 310 396 2870
F. +1 310 396 0399
www.dagandesign.com

DURAVIT
Duravit USA, Inc.
1750 Breckinridge Parkway, suite 500
30096, Duluth GA, USA
Ph. +1 770 931 3575
F. +1 770 931 8454
www.duravit.us

ELMAR CUCINE
Via Emilo Salgari 18
31030 Biancade, Italy
Ph. +39 0422 849 142
www.elmarcucine.com

HORM
Via S. Giuseppe, 25
30082 Azzano Decimo (Pordenone), Italy
Ph. +39 0434 640 733
F. +39 0434 640 735
www.horm.it

IMU DESIGN
Punavuorenkatu 20 E 47
00150 Helsinki, Finland
Ph. +358 50 585 7399
F. +358 9 622 4361
www.imudesign.org

KABALAB
311 Baltic Street, suite 1ª
11201 Brooklyn NY, USA
Ph. +1 718 666 5683
F. +1 718 935 1080
www.kabalab.com

LAGO
Lago Spa
Via dell'Artigianato II 21
35010 Villa del Conte, Italy
Ph. +39 049 5994 299
F. +39 049 5994 191
www.lago.it

MASSIEOFFICE
www.massieoffice.com

MB STUDIO - SISTEMA MIDI
Carrer del Puig 12
08510 Roda de Ter, Spain
Ph. +34 938 500 038
F. +34 938 500 245
www.sistema-midi.com

MDF
Via Morimondo 5/7
20143 Milan, Italy
Ph. +39 02 8180 4100
F. +39 02 8180 4108/09
www.mdfitalia.it

PORRO
Porro Industria Mobili SRL
Via per Cantù 35
22060 Montesolaro, Italy
Ph. +39 031 780 237
F. +39 031 781 529
www.porro.com

RAFEMAR
Pol. Bufalvent
Ap. Correos 98
Miquel Servet 40-42
08240 Manresa, Spain
Ph. +34 938 784 810
F. +34 938 745 014
www.rafemar.com

SAWAYA & MORONI
Via Andegari 18
20121 Milan, Italy
Ph. +39 02 8639 5218
F. +39 02 8646 4831
www.sawayamoroni.com

SUB-ZERO
The Westye Group | Europe Ltd
6B Imprimo Park, Lenthall Road
Debden, Loughton
IG10 3UF Essex, UK
Ph. +44 20 8418 3800
F. +44 20 8418 3899
www.subzero.com

VIABLE LONDON
112 Cremer Business Centre
37 Cremer Street
London E2 8HD, UK
Ph. +44 207 729 4144
www.viablelondon.com

VICCARBE
Viccarbe Hábitat S.L.
Trav. Camí el Racó 1
Pol. Norte Beniparrell
46469 Valencia, Spain
Ph. +34 961 201 010
F. +34 961 211 211
www.viccarbe.com

VINÇON
Passeig de Gràcia 96
08008 Barcelona, Spain
Ph. +34 932 156 050
F. +34 932 155 037
www.vincon.com

VITRA
Vitra Inc.
29 9th Avenue
10014 New York NY, USA
Ph. +1 212 463 5700
F. +1 212 929 6424
www.vitra.com

WILDWOOD CREATIONS INC
Ph. +1 646 228 1943
Ph. +1 646 621 4934
www.wildwoodcreationsinc.com

WOGG
Im Grund 16
5405 Baden-Dättwil, Switzerland
Ph. +41 56 4833 700
F. +41 56 4833 719
www.wogg.ch

ZANOTTA
Via Vittorio Veneto 57
20054 Nova Milanese, Italy
Ph. +39 0362 4981
F. +39 0362 451 038
www.zanotta.it